HONORING THE VOID

Sept, 3, 2013
To Kelly,
May you find peace
and consolation in these pages.

Joe Veneron

HONORING THE VOID

Meditations on the Meaning of Life from MARYKNOLL *Magazine*

Joseph R. Veneroso, M.M.

ORBIS BOOKS
Maryknoll, New York 10545
www.orbisbooks.com

ORBIS BOOKS
Maryknoll, New York 10545

Fathers and Brothers
MARYKNOLL™

Founded in 1970, Orbis Books endeavors to publish works that enlighten the mind, nourish the spirit, and challenge the conscience. The publishing arm of the Maryknoll Fathers and Brothers, Orbis seeks to explore the global dimensions of the Christian faith and mission, to invite dialogue with diverse cultures and religious traditions, and to serve the cause of reconciliation and peace. The books published reflect the views of their authors and do not represent the official position of the Maryknoll Society. To learn more about Maryknoll and Orbis Books, please visit our website at www.maryknollsociety.org.

Library of Congress Cataloging-in-Publication Data

Veneroso, Joseph R.
  Honoring the void : meditations on the meaning of life from Maryknoll magazine / Joseph R. Veneroso, M.M.
    pages cm.
  ISBN 978-1-62698-026-6 (pbk.)
1. Life—Religious aspects—Christianity—Meditations. I. Title.
  BT696.V46 2013
242—dc23
                          2012050002

TABLE OF CONTENTS

INTRODUCTION

The title, *Honoring the Void*, the second collection of my photo reflections from MARYKNOLL magazine, comes from the poem of the same name that received an overwhelmingly favorable response from readers. Many have asked and received permission to reprint this reflection and include it in memorial services. As we age, we lose beloved family and friends. Our own mortality looms ever larger. What would I like to tell people who gather to mourn me after I die? What words would I like to hear from a loved one who is now gone? I believe this poem touches so many hearts because it springs from our most common and shared human experience.

Human life, in all its glorious messiness, underpins not only each reflection in this anthology, but also our Christian belief in the Incarnation. From manger to cross, Christ consecrates and unites humanity with himself as well as with the created universe. Some poems invite the reader to find God in mundane experiences; others lift our thoughts heavenward to celebrate our ability to witness the glory of creation and respond, "Wow!"

It is this mysterious ability humans have, not just to observe but also to appreciate and celebrate creation that separates us from other living things; paradoxically it is the same spirit that then unites us with all that is.

With this in mind, the poems examine various facets of human existence, as well as our beautiful religious traditions, to savor sublime truths hidden within them and within us. Above all, this collection of meditations strives to re-present gospel values in such a way that the reader recognizes God in simple, everyday circumstances so as to savor today's connection to eternity.

Each poem comes with my prayer that you see yourself and life and God more clearly, and that love overflows your heart, inspiring you to share your joy with others.

THE MEDITATIONS

S. Sprague/Peru

A Prayer for
FAMILIES

*Dear Lord, may every child know
a loving mother's care
a father's wise tenderness and
a sibling's sometimes annoying
way of showing affection.*

*May every mother celebrate
the miracle of life
and have a faithful spouse
with whom to share
daily burdens and joys.*

*May every father provide
a safe place for children to grow
and a warm lap on which to take refuge
against the world.*

Sprague/Peru

Dear God, provide grandchildren with willing ears
to listen to tales of times gone by
and of adventures long past
their grandpas yearn to tell;
And cozy kitchens, too, at grandma's house
where holiday foods and smells have power
to transport memories across the years.

12

Lord, supply a father's love to those
deprived of knowing this on earth
and Mother Mary, come, fill the emptiness
of all who never knew the one who gave them birth.

Jesus, Mary and Joseph, remind us
in times of trouble:
what makes a family holy is not
the absence of problems
but the presence of God.

Amen

13

Blessings in disguise

Photo meditation on the feast of Christ the King
photos by Sean Sprague

Kneel in the presence of our God;
Bow before his holy face.
See the glory of the Lord,
  Veiled within the human race.

Angels tremble at the thought
of praising divine majesty
not revealed through mystic garb
but through our human tapestry.

All hail then to the King of Kings
who dwells beyond the farthest skies
yet who favors all who see
his holy blessings in disguise.

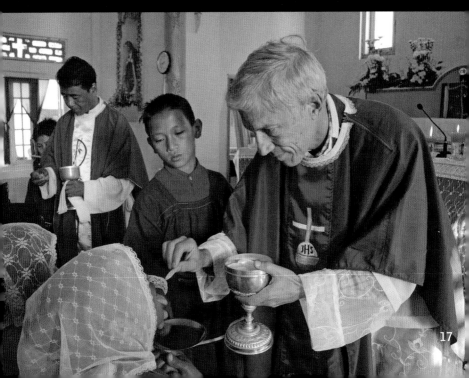

S. Sprague/Peru

I laud the grass that becomes the hay to make the straw.
I praise the tree offering its wood to become the manger.
I honor the donkey bearing a family to safe haven.
I sing of a distant star guiding seekers to the truth.
I extol the righteous man who protects God's precious gift.
I bless the maiden who brought the Light to the light.

See! Each has a unique role to play on this most holy night,
The sheep no less than the angelic hosts,
Ovine baas intermingling with celestial Glorias,
Pungent bovine odors offsetting exotic frankincense.
No thing too humble, no station so low
It fails to respond to a higher calling
To become something more sacred, noble and pure.

S. Sprague/Myanmar

S. Sprague/Myanmar

At length all eyes turn to the one who remains
At the same time director, producer and lead character
In the title role of savior of the world, redeemer of humankind,
Word-Made-Flesh and splendor of God Most High:
A weak, wet, wrinkled, tiny, soft, helpless and innocent Baby.

No mistake. No miscasting. This infant's well-rehearsed
Gurgling and cooing reduce the world to silence.
And we, who have for far too long considered ourselves
Mere spectators to be entertained and amused
By this Christmas pageant are shocked when the Child
Turns to gaze at us as if to say, "Now! Speak your lines!
Play the part for which you have been chosen by me!"

Cloud of witnesses

O, cast off the tired, rusty shackles of yesterday
That bind you to lonely shadows of the past.
If memory serves, then let it truly serve
But as a reminder that they who lived and died
For faith, for love, for God
Remain with us still and always will.

Today they walk among us unhaloed, uncanonized, unsung
And yet their lives, their prayers, their countless sacrifices
Surround us in our hour of need, uphold our cause,
Intercede on our behalf, keep us safe
And fill our emptiness with God's grace
As they draw down heaven's daily benediction.

MARY, OUR MOTHER

JOHN THE BAPTIST

Look! A second Francis of Assisi, there, waiting to catch a bus.

Another Joan of Arc, there, in the supermarket checkout line.

Ignatius, too, come again, now stuck in a traffic jam.

Therese, sitting on a park bench. Dominic, washing windows.

And what of you? How will you join this sacred company?

With quiet prayer or unassuming service?

A gentle touch or bold witness to the truth?

Do not just venerate the saints; be one!

Sanctify the simple things of life

And take part in tomorrow's litany.

DOROTHY DAY/U.S.

JOSEPHINE BAKHITA/SUDAN

PADRE PRO/MEXICO

Clues to
Mission

E. Wheater/Peru

Mirrors magnify the light

And dispel the darkness by

Reflecting God's love to hearts

Yearning for both bread and truth.

Knowing peace follows justice and

Not counting the cost, we go

Offering to everyone on earth

Love beyond all telling and

Life to the fullest in Christ.

S. Sprague/Tanzania

Prayer, penance and patience bring

Renewal and reconciliation of

Old enemies and former friends.

Christ's Cross conquers hate by

Love and replaces doubt with

Answers from humble hearts

Inspired to leave all for Jesus' sake.

Mission means going away for now

So as to come to our eternal home.

Jesus shows and is the Way

Unlocking prison doors by

Sharing knowledge, wisdom and time

To knock down cruel barriers and build

Instead, bridges between peoples for

Christ's kingdom here on

Earth.

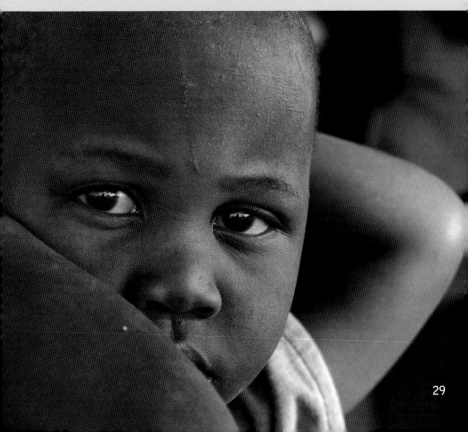

Come to God, go to the world

Photo meditation on vocations

CNS photo/B. Roller/U.S.

Come to me, you with broken, mended hearts
who know the pain and joy and confusion
of love and life.
Come with your wounds and scars and failures
for from these shall flow patience, courage
and strength.
Come with your experiences no less than your education
for wisdom springs more from how you live
than from who you are or what you know.

CNS photo/A. Waguih/Egypt

Come with the rock-hard stubbornness of Peter
and the missionary zeal of Paul.
Come with the loyal love of Mary Magdalene
and the undying friendship of Lazarus.
Come with the natural poetry of Francis
and the visionary leadership of Joan.
Come with the childlike simplicity of Bernadette
and the doubt-plagued faith of Mother Teresa.
Come.

31

Go out to the farthest corners of the world.
Go to the least, the lowest and the loneliest.
Go reveal the riches hidden among the poor.
Go give health to the sick,
and comfort to those who mourn.

S. Sprague/Guatemala

Go with the fire of the Magnificat
burning within your heart
and the Body of Christ alive
within your soul's tabernacle.
Go break down the barriers dividing my people.
Go tear down the walls of ignorance and fear.
Go lift up the fallen and raise up the weak.
Go with the Spirit to sustain you.

Come and go! I am with you always.
The reign of God is at hand!
See! I give you my Word!

DAYSTAR OF
HOLY JOY

O. Duran/Mexico

When Gabriel upset the Virgin's plans
With unsettling news as simple as it was profound;
When Joseph misunderstood and insisted
On a donkey ride to Bethlehem;
When a frazzled innkeeper offered a stable
As a makeshift maternity ward;
Amidst sweet-smelling hay and warm cattle,
In between labor pains,
Shining in the deepest night
Behold! The daystar of holy joy!

O. Duran/Me[x]

Clutching the Child closely to her bosom
As they fled Herod's madness,
Mary and Joseph sought shelter and safety,
Strangers in a foreign land.
Anxiously they later sought what they feared lost
Relieved and confused at finding the One who never left.
Yet through it all and especially there
On that lonely hill when all hope seemed gone
Content to wait for the morning light
Confident in the ultimate victory
Even in the midst of bitter defeat
Dark grief gave birth to eternal joy.

Amid life's disappointments and heartaches
Look and you will see it shining from afar
This star of joy which no one can take away
Nor any amount of sorrow diminish.
Though battles be many and failures abound
Know that the war has already been won
And we are closer to that Day when
God grants true peace to all people of good will
Hope to all who dwell on Earth
And holy joy to the world.

Defiant hope

O. Duran/Ker

Amid mourning and too many tears
Unknown, little noticed,
Seed from a funeral wreath falls to the ground and dies.
Buried and blanketed by snow, forgotten,
It too rests for a time in peace.
Then one April day, there soft upon last year's grave
A single blossom spreads petals of defiant hope:
New life from yesterday's wounds.

S. Sprague/China

When your shattered dreams lie in ruins
Like so much smoldering rubble
From battles fought and lost
See! From its unlikely mausoleum,
Bearing no likeness whatsoever to what lay there entombed,
Hope emerges, spreads its wings victorious o'er the cocoon,
Glorious, triumphant and altogether new

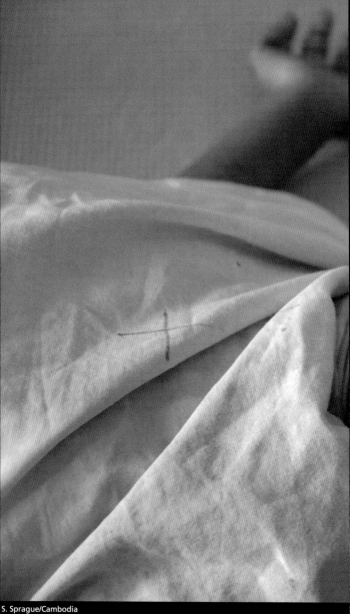

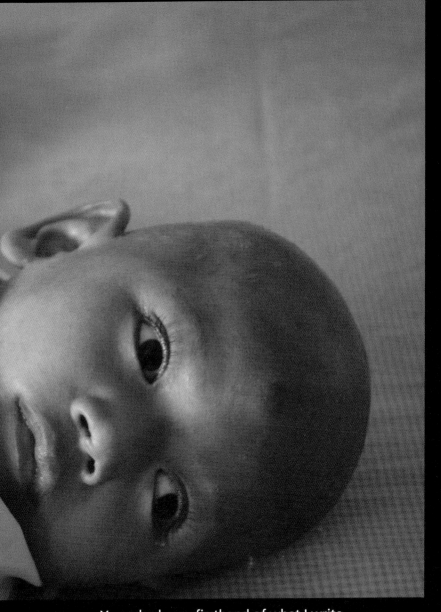

You who know firsthand of what I write
Announce to all peoples burdened and confused
Who may have lost faith in a merciful God,
Be yourselves living proof
How everyday blessings reveal eternal truths.
Each newborn baby bears good news to a war-weary world:
For all our failures, faults and selfishness
God still believes in us.

Dignity redefined

Photo meditation on human work

With grace and poise unsurpassed
by bejeweled heads of state
and with more patience
than enlightened monks
she waits and waits
for discounted courtesy
of strangers.

S. Sprague/Chile

43

Bundled burdens borne like precious cargo,
they struggle on.

O. Duran/Kenya

Heedless of social class she knows
others have more need of her wares than she of theirs.

S. Sprague/Boliv

This Michelangelo of the earth carves hardened soil
using only muscled sweat and iron resolve.
With greater pride than when
the Master revealed David's glory

he harvests
a simple crop
and boasts to
all the world:
"This is mine."

45

S. Sprague/Japan

GLORIOUS DIMINISHMENT
A Lenten meditation on aging

Autumn splendor of the leaf whose life
appears all but past and yet
there, in its final days, reveals a glory
heretofore hidden by its youth.

Stained and pungent from harvests past
only when the winepress crushes grapes
can life's fermentation yield
a choice and worthy vintage.

Sprague/Bolivia

So do not fear or fret
when youth passes and beauty fades
as they always have and surely will.
Memory, too, may well grow dim with time
and strength diminish in due course.
Forget all else but remember this:
A deeper strength, an inner beauty
will emerge, as a statue
from the living rock
chipped and polished by the Sculptor's hand.

48

© Duran/Egypt

But should wisdom not come with age
and time and illness rob a once
proud and noble frame of all comeliness;
should humor fail, kindness flee
and even hope and faith take flight
then, even then, especially then
recall how from the ruins of fallen humanity
a Savior rose and will return
and in the flesh we too will one day
rise and ascend.

Photo reflection on the Incarnation,

God knows

God knows how it feels

To cry like a baby and die like a criminal.

God knows how it feels

To work with rough hands on rougher wood

And walk this earth with calloused feet

And taste the sweetness of precious food

Shared one last time with parting friends.

God knows a broken heart hurts more

Than whip or cross or nails or crown.

God knows comfort in a mother's arms,

Longing for a father's love,

Sadness at a brother's loss,

Strength of a sister's undying loyalty.

God knows why

A heart overflowing with love

Erupts with anger

When people hurt one another.

God knows the joy of life restored

When the dead arise and the lost are found.

God knows all this not by being God alone

But because a woman once said yes

And God became one of us.

Here I stand

You filled my heart with glowing visions of a world
Where justice, truth, goodness and beauty coexist,
Where right triumphs and evil fails,
Where children live loved, fed, clothed and taught
What bad there is need not forever be,
Where laughter marks unfettered, unworried youth
Unaware all that is good might soon be no more

J.J.Beeching/Myanmar

And the aged pass each precious, fleeting hour
With grace and quiet dignity.

You filled my mind with images of peace
On earth still sundered by war, violence and strife
While anxious hands grope for tools or weapons
Though plowshares lack for want of still unbeaten swords.

55

S. Sprague/Mexico

Then you dared me keep silent if I could
In the face of our world's self-inflicted wounds
(What chance did I have against your Word
the universe itself cannot contain?)
Knowing I had the power to change the world
By starting with myself
I began to speak, to tell of all I knew and dreamed and believed
But if I could not, then I stood content

Duran/El Salvador

To let some simple deed become a paving stone
In the highway leading to our God.

Yes, many misunderstand and others doubt
And some threaten me with death—or worse
But here I stand, I can do no other,
For while I live, each man and woman is
My favorite sister and my long-lost brother. 57

S. Sprague/Namibia

Photo meditation on life lessons

One who listens without judgment

And hears without disdain

Whose gentle guidance employs neither guilt nor fear

And who regards each fault or failure

Not with disappointment, ridicule, anger or hurt

But with that rare compassion that flows

From knowing an invaluable, albeit painful, lesson has been learned.

How best to survive—no—thrive in a less than perfect world

And forgive, yield, succeed or totally botch things up

With equal grace and dignity

S. Sprague/Bolivia

Regarding the world with wonder

And people with utmost respect

Teaching along the way, almost by chance,

This most precious, sublime and—yes—holy of life's lessons:

How to be truly, fully, human

Without embarrassment or excuse

Imitating, perhaps unknowingly, the One who came

Lived, died and rose again

As mentor to us all

And in so doing saved the world.

S. Sprague/Kenya

Home to Paradise

Of death and sin destroy the gloom.

His tears sufficed to pay the price

To call us back to Paradise.

64

Prague/China

A new day dawns, our sins are gone,

Our exile at an end.

For Easter means the time has come

HONORING
THE VOID

O. Duran/Mexico

Do not mourn this joyous lump of earth I have become.
O shed a tear or two, if you must, for our time now ended,
for dreams unrealized and hopes unfulfilled.
Yet know the love and life we shared remain.
Even as do you. For a time.

In memory of me, live to the fullest,
for one minute of mindfulness
echoes more than a decade
of mindless busyness.

S. Sprague/Namibia

As for me, I go on to my next adventure.

Confident the smallest atom in the farthest galaxy
obeys God's command,
how can we, made of billions of atoms,
ever be forgotten?
The One who fashioned us from stardust and seashells
and breathed in us a living spirit,
creates, comforts and calls us still
to rise higher and become more.

S. Sprague/Br

And so, despite the emptiness, honor the void
in tribute to what once was;
Bless the pain, as proof it was real and
Light a candle of prayer in the quiet chapel of your soul
to dispel this hour's darkness.

And only when you are ready, let go of even this.
Do not be afraid. I shall live on in your heart
as you do in mine
and as we do in God's.

Seek me in the sunrise or in the pounding surf.
See me in the autumn leaves or
hear me howling in the wintry storm.
Then you will know, as I now do,
how yesterday's death
gives birth to eternal tomorrow.

HYMN
TO OUR
ALIEN GOD

O LORD, WHO KNEW NO PEACE ON EARTH
From the first moment of your birth
Escaping from your native home
    AND IN A FOREIGN LAND TO ROAM
WITH FAMILY FEARING FOR YOUR LIFE
    Amidst a world of pain and strife

Announcing to all who would hear,
"Repent! The reign of God is near!"
To seek and find and save the lost

You built your kingdom here on earth
And on the cross you paid the cost
To show all people their true worth.

73

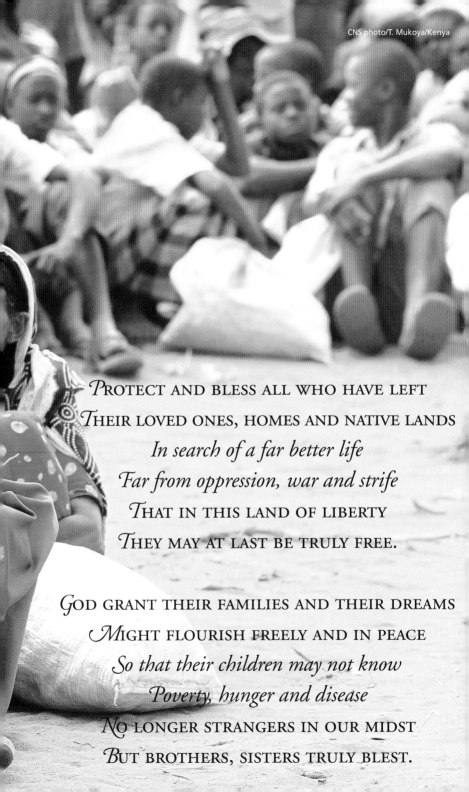

CNS photo/T. Mukoya/Kenya

Protect and bless all who have left
Their loved ones, homes and native lands
In search of a far better life
Far from oppression, war and strife
That in this land of liberty
They may at last be truly free.

God grant their families and their dreams
Might flourish freely and in peace
So that their children may not know
Poverty, hunger and disease
No longer strangers in our midst
But brothers, sisters truly blest.

CNS photo/J. Roberts, Reuters/U.S.

Litany of freedom

Because of them we stand here free
To speak out or keep silence.
Free from fear and want and poverty
Free to choose and free to go our own way.

O blessed freedom first bestowed
On poor, forgotten slaves in Egypt's land
O frightful freedom of the wilderness
When we were forced to rely on God alone
O eternal freedom purchased for all time
By the blood of Christ on the cross
Which broke once and for all
The chains that bound us to the past.

CNS photo/M. Rossi, Reuters/Italy

S. Sprague/Tanzania

O holy freedom, which compels us
To go out to all still enslaved to sin,
Society or self and show the Way
To enter into and live new life
As precious sons and daughters of God.

79

MINDING ONE'S BUSINESS

PHOTO MEDITATION ON LABOR

Amid the myriad hurrying, nameless
Commuters and travelers
Ever so eager to get someplace else
I saw him there out of the corner of my eye
Against an out-of-the-way wall
At the entrance to Grand Central Terminal.

He had a shoeshine stand
With customers enthroned above
Like monarchs and potentates
Or at least like people important enough
To pay to have their footwear polished.

81

K. Thomas/Peru

He was an older man by the looks of his gray hair
But his smile made him seem eternally young.
I watched transfixed as he shined each shoe
With the attention, devotion and talent
Of a Michelangelo and with no less pride
In his accomplishments.

Never before or since have I seen such total dedication
To the task at hand, nor such absolute absorption
As if, unlike all the others, he indeed was
Exactly where he wanted to be and
Doing exactly what he wanted to do.

Then I saw his patrons put aside their Times
To chat awhile with this common laborer
As if, in his own quiet way and by minding his own business
He had already attained what they so desperately sought.

E. Wheater/Nicaragua

Many years have passed since that day and perhaps so has he
Who transformed his work into a labor of love.
Still he remains forever in my heart to inspire me
To do even the simplest, most menial and boring task
With complete satisfaction and surrender
And to thank him and share his memory with you
Thus granting him a small measure of immortality.

MYSTERY IN THE FLESH

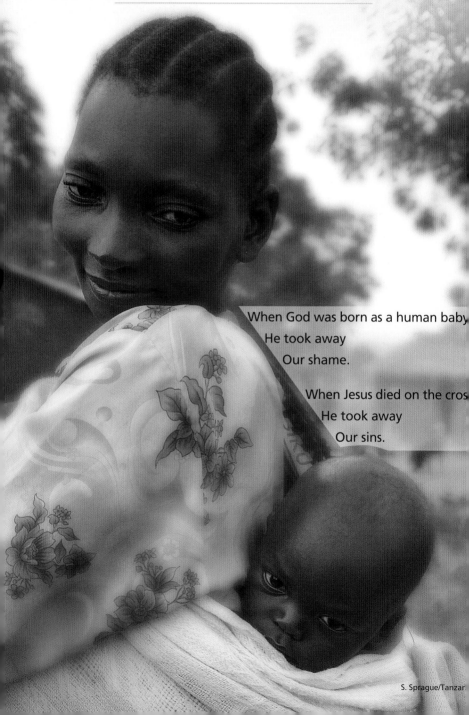

When God was born as a human baby
He took away
Our shame.

When Jesus died on the cros
He took away
Our sins.

S. Sprague/Tanzar

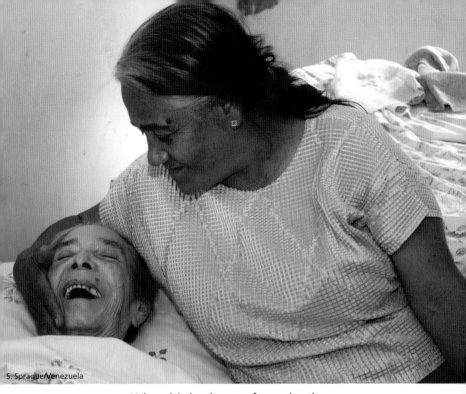

S. Sprague/Venezuela

When his body rose from death
He took away
Our fear.

And when he ascended bodily into heaven
He took away
Our excuses.

S. Sprague/Nicaragua

When the Holy Spirit descended upon us
We received
Dignity to replace our shame,
Grace in place of our sins,
Love to cast out all fears,
And courage to live this Good News.

See! We become the living Temple
Of the Most Holy Trinity
In bodily form.

Our poor excuse

We choose you who have no choice
but to live from day to day
And speak for you who have no voice
who work long hours for little pay

Sprague/Philippines

We stand with you who cannot stand
   To watch another child die
And hear your stories however banned
      by those who do not hear your cry.

CNS/F. Omar, Reuters

We walk with you through darkest night
confessing that we too are lost
To let you guide us by your light
and tell your truth, whate'er the cost.

Sprague/Guatemala

We fight for you who cannot win
in life's struggle against these odds
And repent for all in power of sin
who sold their souls to other gods.

We bless you for blessing us
        with your naked honesty
    By teaching all about God, thus
        T'is you in fact who set us free.

Why then, friends, you might well ask
        God long ago this treasure hid
    Would we embark on such a task?
        We choose the poor 'cause Jesus did.

prague/Peru

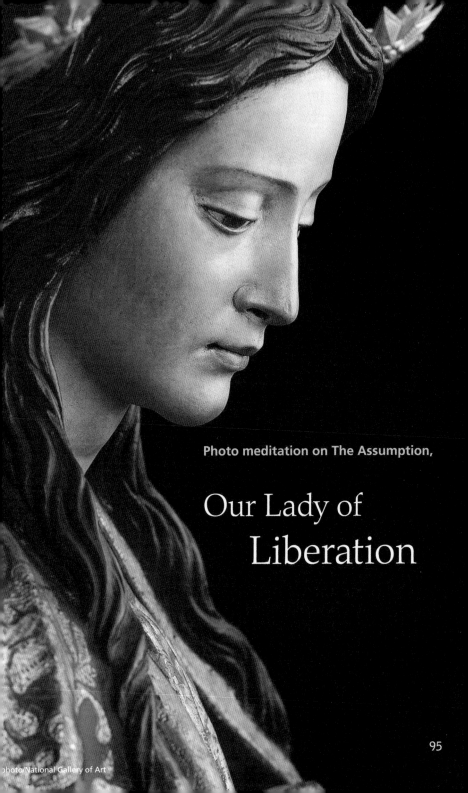

Photo meditation on The Assumption,

Our Lady of Liberation

photo/National Gallery of Art

Hail, blessed woman among all women!
You who shattered the iron grip
Of sin, evil and death
With your simple and humble Yes
To God's most holy Will.

P. Grillo/U.S.

You, who became a living tabernacle,
Gave birth to the true liberator of humankind.
Your Yes to God echoes in the words of your Son
Down through the ages and to every corner of the world.

See how the mighty fall from their thrones
And the lowly rise up from the dust;
Abundant blessings fill the poor
While the powerful go away empty.

CNS photo/A. Giuliani

May our souls like yours always magnify the Lord
To rouse the downtrodden and stir faith to action
Till the reign of God extends to every heart
And every life finds in Christ, your Son and our God,
The source and summit of eternal freedom.

PRAYER FOR JUSTICE

Most merciful, almighty and just God
Mingled with the blood of Jesus,
the blood of our sisters and brothers
cries out all the more to you from the earth
and shakes the very gates of heaven.

Open our ears to hear the cry of the poor
amplified by the voice of your Son on the cross
and turn our hearts to help the oppressed
as they daily mount the slopes of Calvary.

that we might look upon the world
and see what you see.

Let us never be frightened by the shadow of evil
nor silenced by the threats of the powerful
nor overwhelmed by the task at hand.

CNS/F. Spotorno/Venezuela

101

CNS/R. Krause/China

Rather, send your Holy Spirit to steady our hands
and strengthen our voices to speak out boldly
in the name of all that is good and right and just.

Fill our spirits with resolve to establish
your kingdom here on earth.

/Reuters/Israel

Above all let us assault and tear down
barriers between peoples.

Stone by stone help us break down the walls
of ignorance and fear dividing your sons and daughters
and brick by brick help us build bridges
of understanding, forgiveness and peace.

Amen.

Photo reflection on cultural diversity, photos by Sean Sprague
2011 CPA Award Winner Best Poem

Prayer for protection from daisies

Spare me, O Lord, from a garden overrun by only daisies
A lake infested with nothing but trout and swans
A forest where just maple trees grow.

Deliver me, O God, from a world where
Everyone looks like me, talks like me,
Thinks like me and totally agrees with me.

In your infinite wisdom, my Lord and my God,
You fashioned the stars, planets, galaxies
And peoples where no two are alike.

Like the snowflakes that blanket the spinning earth
When seasons change and weather varies,
Everything on earth reflects your wisdom in diversity.

And so I sing your praises, my God, with many voices
Offering all kinds of hymns and songs
Sung in different keys and tempos and harmonies.

I bless your Name and power revealed
Through countless cultures and varied tongues
And different races and beliefs, a sacred symphony,

A veritable garden of splendid humanity
A motley patchwork of people's faces
Creating a holy mosaic to your glory.

PRAYER TO THE GOD OF CREATION
Photo meditation on ecology

Guide our nets, O great river spirit,
So our boat may abound with your bounty.
Draw fish closer and let not our work be in vain.
In gratitude we draw life from your murky depths
That we and our families might live,
Humbly knowing our turn will one day come
To offer ourselves as food for other living things.

CNS photo/Reuters/Bolivia

Bless us, O Mother Earth, as we kneel on and before you.
You, from whom all life springs and to whom all life returns,
Bless us, and others through us, especially our children,
With health, prosperity and happiness.
Let us be ever mindful of your tender care
And never draw a breath without offering thanks
For your generous gifts this day.

Sun, seed and soil combine to yield a rich harvest
Thanks, too, to rains both plentiful and soft.
And thank you, O God of Creation,
For drawing us together on this journey
So we need no longer walk this way alone.
We travel down paths both familiar and unknown
Yet side-by-side our adventure now unfolds.

S Sprague/Tanzania

Teach us, then, O Lord of Everything,
To seek your will, to celebrate your truth,
To savor your Word, to wonder at your great mercy,
To stand in awe of your goodness,
To share your gifts and to enjoy your beauty
Reflected no less in blossoming faces
Than in outbursts of random roses.

Photo meditation for November
photos by Sean Sprague

Remembering
to give thanks

Saints of God, come to our aid
You who stand in the presence of the Most High
Remind us of the glorious things God did through you
And fill us with gratitude for all we have received.

Spirits and souls of the just
Pray for us as we pray for you
Remind us we stand today in thanksgiving
For all relatives and ancestors who have gone before us.

Mother Earth, teach us to treat you with reverence
For from you and through you our Creator God
Gave us our Savior and continues to fill us
With all good things necessary for life.

114

In grateful thanksgiving, we raise our hands in prayer

For all we have, that God might also bless others through us

And that with each memory of God's goodness

Our hearts might overflow with joy. Amen.

Song *of the divine* PHYSICIAN

Photo meditation on healing, photos by Sean Sprague

Maryknoll Sister Aida Manlucu, left, shares the concerns of Magdalena Tjombe in Namibia.

There is One who brings true healing
To the body, mind and soul
Inner truth by faith revealing
Who alone can make us whole.

Serving the divine Physician

To the farthest lands they go
Heedless of the worst conditions
God's true love and mercy show.

See! They come, an army splendid
In our darkest hour of need
When all hope and life seemed ended
From all sorrow we are freed.

Neighbor out to neighbor reaching
Bringing life through healing touch
Singing, praising, helping, teaching
How to live and give so much.

Father Joseph Fedora blesses Daniel, 14, who suffers from cerebral palsy in Brazil.

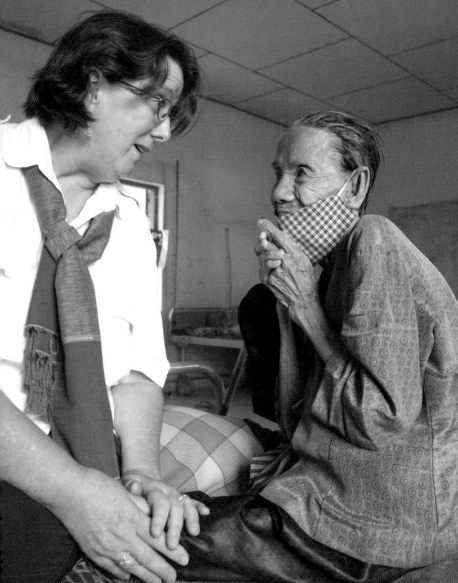

Through his wounds we find salvation
By his stripes we have been healed
Shout Good News to every nation
God's great love has been revealed!

Maryknoll Lay Missioner Adel O'Regan, left, visits
Lin Chou, 84, a tuburculosis patient in Cambodia.

Springtime of promise

Photo meditation on new beginnings

CNS/L. Nicholson, Reuters/U.S.

Not just for ourselves but more for these
Too long forgotten, abandoned and unknown
The silent, the suffering, the insecure
These insignificant bearers of the face of God
Yet for justice too, too long denied
And for elusive peace

S. Sprague/Kenya

No longer willing to accept things as they are
And daring to believe in a better way
Forsaking comfort and sometimes safety
Risking uncertain dangers and all-too-real
Inconveniences, both small and great

They came by twos, by tens, by millions
Enduring hunger, thirst and bitter cold
To be able to say to generations still unborn
I was there that day, standing shoulder to shoulder
With fellow dreamers from around the world ...

121

...WITNESSING
TO HOPE

THE FOURTH COMMANDMENT

S. Sprague/Kenya

He answers to many names: Dad, Daddy, Pop, Pa and, yes, even Father.
He assumes so many faces: giant, ogre, defender, teacher, judge,
provider and, on occasion, friend.
Perhaps absent or too painfully present,
He bears the blame for not remaining perfect in my eyes.
Yet his not "being there for me" does not absolve me
Of my obligation to "be there for him."
Not because he is worthy or deserving, which he may very well be,
But because, for better or worse, I would not be without him.
It's not his fault he unwittingly shares his role with God.
So why do I find it so hard to forgive his getting old?
Do I dread his loss or fear this too real reminder of my own mortality?
Eventually I come to appreciate, for all his faults and virtues,
He was nothing less
Than a man.

And what of her whose heart for nine months beat in sync with mine?
Whose love I felt before she ever held me in her arms?
Who, given a choice, still chose to give me life?
Who loved me enough to let me go?
If any could be at once both virgin and mother, it was she.
Songs she sang to me as a child return to comfort me during difficult times
As if she somehow knew I'd need them during distant, lonely days.
Mind reader, life coach and my chief cheerleader
Who believed in me beyond embarrassment.
One hurt glance from her was often enough to get me to
Reconsider my ways, not that I always did.
Sure, she played the guilt card to the hilt,
Reminding me at every turn the extent of her sacrifice.
While outwardly rebellious I inwardly relished the bond and proudly boast:
"Yup, that's my mom."

S. Sprague/Thailand

So here I am, for better or worse,
A most unlikely combination of these two.
How to honor them so unlike any others to me?
Inscribe their names on cold granite or dedicate
These words to their memory?
Perhaps. But far better still would be to live in such a way
As to justify in my eyes if not the world's
This most singular grace of being their child.

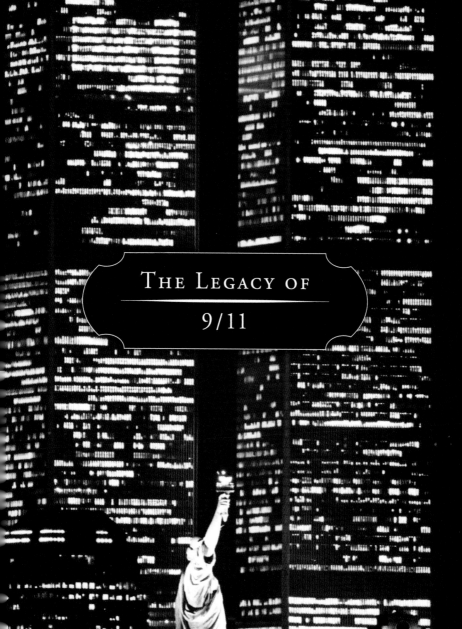

THE LEGACY OF
9/11

Up from the smoking ruins of our shattered innocence
Arose two conflicting spirits of our times:
An angel of goodness and a demon of fear
To battle for America's soul.

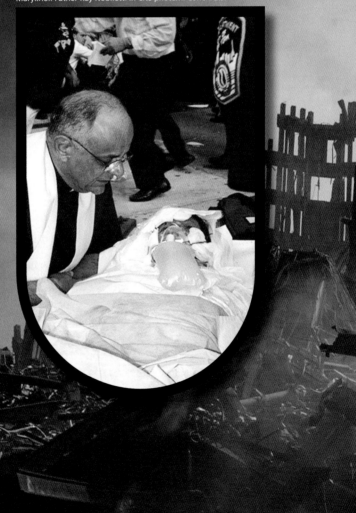

Maryknoll Father Ray Nobiletti in CNS photo/R. Cohen/U.S.

Yet if for every act of cruelty and ignorance
True patriots respond with a hundred deeds of kindness and love
Then we whose hearts broke ten years ago
May still stand triumphant at the doorstep of hope.

CNS/M. Segar/U.S.

And to the young who may not recall that day
When victims' and heroes' blood mingled with our tears
And people from around the globe together mourned our loss
Tell of this last chance to be a beacon to our darkened world.

If we would but renew our pledge to work for justice
And live in peace then our true light would shine brighter
And rise higher than the Towers ever could
Realizing no one on earth can destroy us but ourselves.

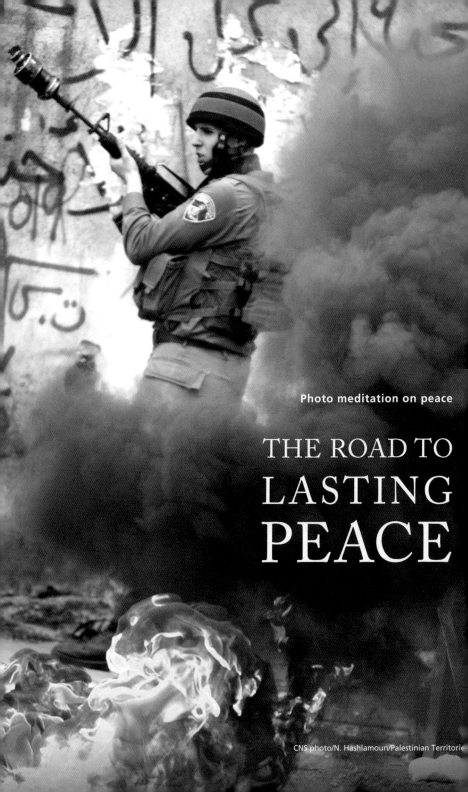

Photo meditation on peace

THE ROAD TO
LASTING
PEACE

CNS photo/N. Hashlamoun/Palestinian Territori

CNS photo/Sri Lanka

Too many false starts, too many dashed hopes
Litter the dead-end street promising peace
By first defeating foes, silencing critics
And overpowering all adversaries

CNS photo/Ivory Coast

Traveling the road to lasting peace demands
Leaving behind our family baggage
Packed with our great-grandparents' grudges
—Useless ballast that keeps our spirit from soaring
Letting go of personal resentments
—Poison we drink in hopes our enemy will die
Slaying the wild beast of sweet revenge
We foolishly caged in our wounded hearts
Till, no longer content with sapping our strength
And feasting on our happiness
it began to devour our soul, our selves.

We cannot ride the road to lasting peace
On an endless cycle of violence and vengeance
Nor can we travel alone.
As we walk that path together
We must take time to fill in all the holes and gaps
And remove the obstacles left by previous travelers
Lest those who come after us stumble and fall.
And with humility and faith in the Prince of Peace
Let us once and for all utterly destroy our enemies
Through the power of forgiveness
By turning them into friends
For only then will we have finally arrived.

TIME IN SYNC

S. Sprague/Mongolia

Oh would that I had but an extra day or even
hour to set things right or make up for so much
wasted time.
I'd live each precious moment to the full
and share with all this miracle called life.

In fact each minute is a blessed moment of grace
a special gift from God squandered on such as me
to do with as I will or not at all.

Ever mindful of the ticking clock I know my days
are numbered as are yours and every living thing's.
And yet buried deep within this illusion of time
and now I detect a hint of eternity.

S. Sprague/Sudan

Father Kenneth F. Thesing in Sudan

Transplanting your heart

Go to a land and language and people unknown
And there, become a child again.
Dependent on the kindness of strangers
For your daily bread or rice or tortilla or ugali.

There you shall put down new roots,
Watered with tears, much sweat and sometimes blood,
Roots nurtured by prayers whispered in the dark
Or shouted at a now suddenly silent God.

S. Sprague/Bolivia

143

S. Sprague/Bolivia

Father Thomas P. Henehan in Bolivia

And just when all seems so pointless and vain
You'll see a smiling face; you'll make a friend
Welcoming you into a larger, loving family,
Grateful for the simple fact that you are there.

And just as the sun begins to rise on your success
You hear faint echoes in your heart
Of that voice that once called and sent you forth
Saying, "Get up and go! It's time to leave again!"

144

Visit *of the* Magi

S. Sprague/Mongolia

Then came wisdom from the East
    guided by a holy star
    searching long in fields afar
    to find the best among the least.

Without a king nor wish to be one
    with only prayers and tales of old
    giving gifts more fine than gold
    they know a treasure when they see one.

Had they time they would have brought one
special thing to honor youth,
        instead they offer you their truth:
        They found a savior when they sought one.

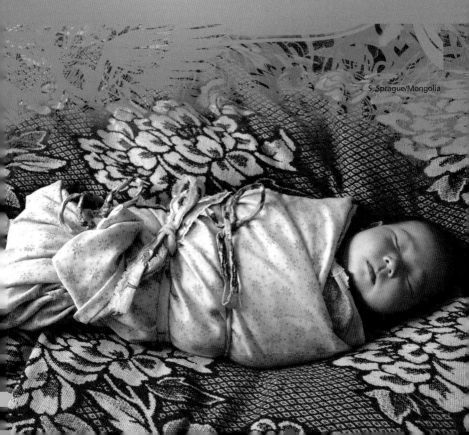

S. Sprague/Mongolia

Who are my Neighbors

Photo meditation

Not just the ones living next door, or down the block
Not just those from my hometown or country
No, my neighbors may or may not look or talk or think like me.
My neighbors may be of another faith or race or political persuasion.
My neighbors are whoever needs my help right now
Whether standing beside me or half a world away

S. Sprague/Peru

But wait, there's more!
My neighbors do not so much need my help as I need theirs.
Without them, I cannot fulfill the law of Christ.
Without them, my worship rings hollow and my prayers
Echo in the emptiness of my heart
Like an abandoned cathedral, cold, dark and deserted

But if I believe God wants me here and now
To bear witness to the truth and announce God's reign
And fulfill God's plan for peace and justice on this earth
Then let my eyes and ears and voice and hands be opened
To see and celebrate and share God's gifts, no matter how small
With whoever needs my meager offering

I NEED FOOD MONEY Home

CNS/P. Jeffrey/U.S.

Then my prayers of praise will be pure
And in the darkest recesses of my soul
A light shall shine in my heart's sanctuary
Keeping vigil before Christ present within.

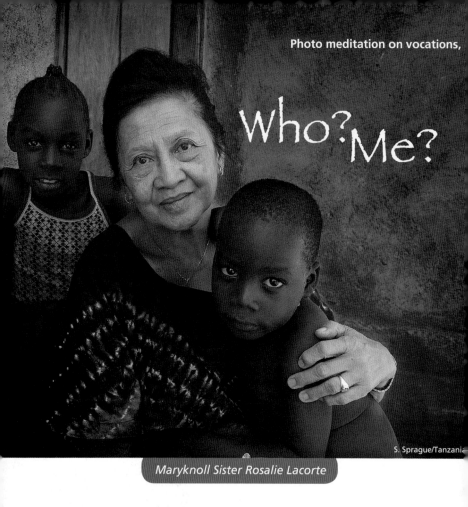

Who? Me?

S. Sprague/Tanzania

Maryknoll Sister Rosalie Lacorte

Yes, you! You, who think your sins too great, your faults too many,
Your talents too few and your words too weak,
You, who feel so small compared to the enormous task at hand,
You, who doubt your faith is strong enough to stand against the powers
And temptations of this present age.
Let your faith in me overcome the doubts in you.

Strive for perfection and holiness but do not wait till their attainment.

The people of the world cannot afford to wait that long.

Somewhere on this earth someone longs to hear

My voice through your lips, my words through your mouth.

Someone waits to know my love, my mercy, my forgiveness

Through your simple willingness to be there.

Maryknoll Lay Missioner Celina Campas

. Sprague/Cambodia

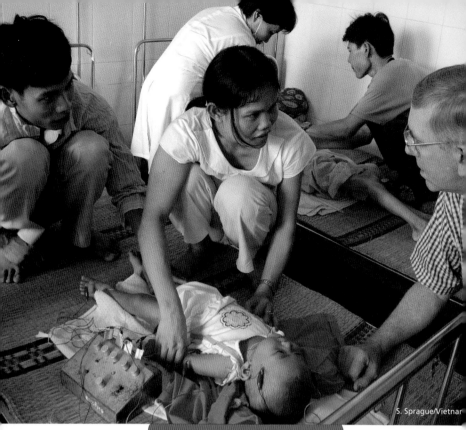

S. Sprague/Vietnar

Maryknoll Father Tom O'Brien

Of course I know your weaknesses.

They make you who and what you are and I love you no less

Nor could I love you any more than when, despite everything,

You try, you fail, you try again. And, at length, you trust

Me who calls you to be with me always, just as I said.

If you believe in me, recall I too believe in you.

I call you by name, I know you by heart.
Everything in your life till now has brought you to this day
For better or worse. Come, then, follow me on the Way
And you will fill your soul's deepest longing. I promise.
Do not be afraid. I will be safe haven in the storm.
So what are you waiting for?

Maryknoll Brother John Beeching

Witness to life
Photo reflection on mission vocation

GO
listen in silence
for truth spoken
in unfamiliar words.

HEAR
laughter no less
than the sound of tears
echoing through walls
of mud or brick or ignoranc

Photos by S. Sprague/Bolivia

SEE
the child, the youth,
the aged and infirm,
and do not fear these
shadows of your former
and future self.

TASTE
the bitter sweet of life.
Drink the cup
down to the dregs.

S. Sprague/Peru

SMELL
the air
heavy with sweat
and incense.

TOUCH
and feel the wounded heart.

Give, love, hope fully.
Then come
bear witness to all
you have heard and seen
tasted and lived.

Tell everyone you meet of
the goodness
and beauty of life
in all its painful glory,
and know that God is here.

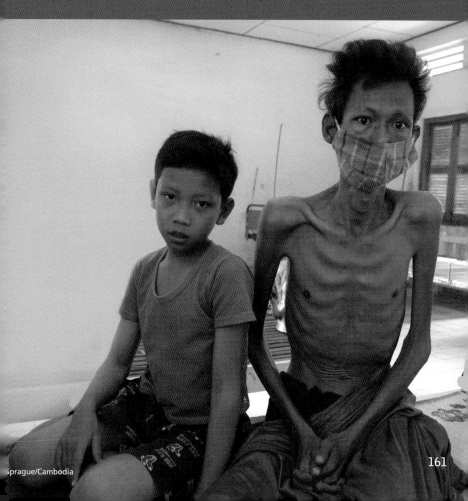

Sprague/Cambodia

Women of the Reign

*When storm clouds cover the earth,
They light candles of hope
Against the impending darkness.*

*At the sound of distant thunder,
They cradle in their arms
Those who tremble at the future.*

S. Sprague/Guatemala

Unshaken by the rumors of war,
They offer a soothing lullaby
To quiet troubled hearts.

And should the earth move,
They stand firm as rocks
Upon which to lean and learn and live.

And when the seas rage,
Their warmth, their smile
Their kindness offer safe harbor.

que/Kenya

The prayers of these women of faith
Pierce the highest heavens
And fly to the very heart of God.

S. Sprague/Taiwan

Their witness goes forth
To the ends of the earth
With visions of a world that might yet be:

S. Sprague/Taiwan

A world of compassion and caring,
Of cooperation and communion
With one another and with all the saints.

ill they transform by their strength of spirit
The tired remnants of our weary world
Into fulfilled promises of God's reign.

Sprague/Kenya

In gratitude

My heartfelt appreciation to all who have encouraged the production of this second anthology of my reflections, notably, Mr. Michael Leach, editor emeritus of Orbis books; Ms. Roberta Savage, head of our art department and her talented staff of artists, Valentín Concha-Núñez, Kimberly Garrrett, Paul Grillo, and John T. Roper, Jr., whose skill and vision helped create this visually appealing collection of photos and poems.

About the Author

Father Joseph Veneroso, M.M., is a Maryknoll priest and former editor of MARYKNOLL magazines, where his photo meditations continue to appear. He is the author of several books through Orbis: *God in Unexpected Places*, *Good News for Today*, and *Mirrors of Grace*, the spirit and spiritualities of the Maryknoll Fathers and Brothers. His first novel, *The Chimera*, a religious murder mystery, is available online through Amazon.com.

Maryknoll Missioners appearing in *Honoring the Void*

Maryknoll Father Lawrence D. Radice, pages 17 (bottom) and 23 (lower right); Maryknoll Sister Dr. Mary Lou Daoust, page 24 (top, left); Maryknoll Sisters Rosalie Lacorte and Mary Reese, page 25 (top, left and center); Maryknoll Father Joyalito F. Tajonera, page 26; Maryknoll Father James J. Madden, page 27; Maryknoll Father Hung M. Dinh, page 28; Maryknoll Father Thomas J. Dunleavy, page 55; Maryknoll Brother Mark A. Gruenke, page 59; Maryknoll Father Philip W. Mares, page 61 (left); Maryknoll Sister Bibiana Bunuan, page 67; Maryknoll Father Kenneth J. Sullivan, page 79 (right); Maryknoll Father James Eble, page 111; Maryknoll Sister Aida Manlucu, page 116; Maryknoll Father Joseph Fedora, page 118; Maryknoll Lay Missioner Adel O'Regan, page 119; Maryknoll Father Raymond J. Nobiletti, page 130; Maryknoll Father Kenneth F. Thesing, page 142; Maryknoll Father Thomas P. Henehan, page 144; Maryknoll Sister Rosalie Lacorte, page 154; Maryknoll Lay Missioner Celina Campas, page 155; Maryknoll Father Thomas J. O'Brien, page 156; Maryknoll Brother John J. Beeching, page 157; Maryknoll Father Kyungsu Son, page 160